KT-371-716

Our Christian Heritage

Marshall Morgan and Scott

Marshall Morgan & Scott
3 Beggarwood Lane,
Basingstoke,
Hants,
RG23 7LP, UK

Designed and produced for
Marshall Morgan & Scott
by Three's Company
12 Flitcroft St,
London WC2

St David's Cathedral, Dyfed.

Paperback ISBN 0 551 01131 9
Hardback ISBN 0 551 01134 3

Set by The Grange Press,
Butts Road, Southwick, Sussex.

Printed in Great Britain by
Redwood Burn, Trowbridge,
Wilts

Foreword

This book brings before us the stirring story of men and women of faith who have through the centuries profoundly influenced our history.

Almost every aspect of life in our islands has been affected by our Christian Heritage – our system of government, justice, education, concern for the social outcast, the deprived and the disadvantaged.

Christian Heritage is not about decaying buildings and crumbling documents – but about the innumerable men and women who down the ages have transformed our island story by their vital Christian faith.

This book graphically records something of this extra-ordinarily rich inheritance.

+GRAHAM LONDIN:
12th March 1984

St Paul's Cathedral, London.

Admiralty Arch, Whitehall, London.

Introduction

Sir Arthur Bryant C.H.

The most important of all the many invaders of our island, and those who had the greatest influence on our history, were the handful who came, not like the fierce Celts, Saxons, Danes and Normans, with long-boat, fire and sword, but who arrived on our shores armed only with a cross, and the faith and courage which that cross gave. They brought Christ's gentle creed of love and sacrifice, and the revolutionary belief, inherent in Christianity, that every individual is a potential soul of equal value in the eyes of God, with a right to be respected and to live his life in his own way. It is this belief in the sanctity of the individual, and of the Christian creed and ethic, which has shaped the ideals of the English – and British – and, with them, by and large, their history. Obstinate, self-righteous, as are all peoples, and often as individuals aggressive, quarrelsome, and greedy, yet in their corporate capacity returning again and again to the inner beliefs of a Christian nation.

For Britain is a Christian land, and only by contemplating her long Christian history can one comprehend her.

Jedburgh Abbey is one of Scotland's most impressive medieval buildings.

Jedburgh Abbey was damaged and burned by the English in the sixteenth century.

Our history has been forged by the actions of many ordinary men and women, whose ideals and beliefs both shaped their lives and touched the lives of others for generations to come. This book is about a handful of those people who, through their faith in God, helped shape our island heritage, our Christian Heritage.

The fall of Rome

Christianity reached the shores of Britain during the Roman period. St Alban (c 250) is the first recorded British martyr and in 314 AD British bishops were delegates to a church conference in France. Archaeological evidence in the mosaic from the Roman villa at Hinton St Mary, Dorset, and the chapel wall painting from Lullingstone, Kent (both to be seen in the British Museum) bear witness to well-established Christianity by 350 AD.

When the Roman legions left these shores, pagan Angles and Saxons invaded from the east and the British believers were steadily driven back into the Welsh mountains.

Patrick

But not all was retreat. The Welshman Patrick was born around 390 AD. His father and grandfather had been Christian priests and he was brought up in their faith. Then, at sixteen, he was captured and taken as a slave to Ireland. After a few years he escaped but felt compelled to go back as a missionary to his former captors.

Westminster Abbey, London. It is here that the monarch is crowned.

St David's Cathedral, Dyfed, South Wales.

Peaceful invasion

One hundred years later a young man fled from his native Christian Ireland. He was the son of an Ulster lord and had spent his youth in the monastery and school of Clonard. This young man's name was Columba.

　　He set out with only twelve other men in 563, and landed on the island of Iona, a mere fragment of land three miles long. Yet from this rocky outcrop Columba achieved the conversion to

Christianity of heathen Scotland and established the Celtic church there.

Iona itself is a gem of natural beauty and planted on it is the abbey Columba founded, now restored by the Iona Community. The island remains today a centre of devotional work and many modern pilgrimages.

The influence of Iona soon spread beyond Scotland. Oswald, king of Northumbria, fled his throne and while exiled in Scotland encountered evangelists from Iona. King once more, Oswald invited Iona to send missionaries to Northumbria, and so Aidan came to Lindisfarne Island in 633. Since Aidan was not fluent in English, King Oswald himself interpreted the Word of God to his thanes and earls.

Iona Abbey has been restored in recent years.

St Martin's cross, Iona.

Not Angles, but Angels

The year of Columba's death, 597, was also the year when, at the opposite end of the country, and surely unknown to any on Iona, another Christian missionary landed on the Isle of Thanet in Kent.

Augustine had been sent by Pope Gregory to carry the Christian message to the land of the Angles and Saxons. The story has it that, when a young man, Gregory had seen some of these fair-haired tribesmen on sale in a Roman slave market. Struck by their appearance, Gregory inquired who they were. On being told they were Angles, he replied: 'Not Angles but Angels.' The impression remained vivid, and through this seemingly chance encounter the idea of a mission to England was born.

There was need for it; surviving Christians, descended from those whose faith arose towards the end of Roman rule in Britain, had been pushed away to Cornwall, Wales and Cumbria by invading Germanic tribes.

'Adoration of the Magi' a panel from the Poor Man's Bible window in the north aisle of the quire, Canterbury Cathedral. The stained glass dates from the thirteenth century.

Converts in Kent

The south porch, Canterbury Cathedral, Kent.

This was a time when no one king could claim to rule over all England. Ethelbert was King of Kent; he was no Christian, but his French queen Bertha was. Through her persuasion the king presented Augustine with a centre in Canterbury – the Chapel of St Martin, an old Romano–British church building.

It must have been an impressive sight, in those far-off pagan days, for the Saxon workers to have watched and listened in wonder as, preceded by a large silver cross, Augustine and his followers made their way to Canterbury, reciting as they went the new, and as yet unfamiliar, Christian prayers.

Worship and evangelism went hand-in-hand; Augustine's powerful sermons were soon drawing massive and receptive crowds. Before long the king himself and thousands of his people had adopted the Christian faith.

No cathedral in Britain is today more renowned than Canterbury. But the site looked very different in Augustine's day, for it was here that he built the first simple church – Christ Church – setting an example for Christians ever since to build a living tribute to God's glory in words, music, paint and stone. Augustine sent out his missionaries throughout the land to spread the good news, and to make contact again with the British Christians in Wales.

He died only about ten years after landing in Kent; a stone cross near Minster on the Isle of Thanet marks his landing. But in that one decade, Augustine of Canterbury had re-kindled the Christian faith in England.

An English poet

We move north again and thirty years after Aidan first came to Lindisfarne, Abbess Hilda of Whitby recognised in Caedmon, a local cowherd, a wonderful gift of poetry. Taken on as a lay-brother he set many Bible stories to verse and songs, which can still be seen carved on stone crosses to this day.

> The creator's power and wisdom
> The deeds of the Father of Glory
> How He, being God eternal
> Was author of all wonders,
> Who first to the songs of men
> Made Heaven for the roof of their abode
> And then created the earth
> Almighty Guardian of Mankind!

– a Caedmon song translated into modern English.

The Venerable Bede

A few years before Caedmon died (c 675) was born the boy who became known to history as the Venerable Bede.

Bede spent his entire life from the age of seven (he did not die till 735) in the monasteries of Wearmouth and Jarrow. It seems to have been a life of devotion, with much prayer and Christian teaching, and scholarship. Bede studied the sciences, the Word of God and wrote a famous *Ecclesiastical History of the English Nation*, the source for the famous story of Gregory and the slave boys. Bede's last few hours on this earth saw the completion of a life-long task, an Anglo-Saxon translation of St John's Gospel.

Bede's was a limited, local life – or so it seems – but from Jarrow, on the edge of the then-known world, his writings spread through the whole of Europe.

It was British pioneers such as Boniface (680-754) from Crediton, Devon – known as the 'apostle to the Germans' – who bore the Christian faith to northern Germany. Boniface had a general commission from the pope to convert anyone anywhere: a job he set about with enormous energy and ingenuity.

Parochial matters

By the time of Bede's death, there had quietly begun one of the central features of Christian life in Britain – the system of parish churches. This system has helped mould the character of the church in Britain and formed one of its most enduring strengths.

In the early years, the cathedral churches were centres for missionary work, and the parish churches formed branches of these missions. At this time, towns barely existed and country parishes were built by local lords, bishops and ordinary people. The parish church, along with the manor house and mill, became the focal point of village life for centuries to come. The tower itself, the most distinctive feature of the English church and English countryside, was probably a Saxon form of 'early warning system' against the threat of Danish invasion.

'Adam delving', a fifteenth-century stained glass panel in St Mary Magdalene Church, Mulbarton, Norfolk.

The celtic cross at Carew, Dyfed.

Painting on the walls

The tower remains a familiar feature of many of our parish churches; less familiar would be the interior of churches of those days. For not until the sixteenth century were the walls of our churches finished in the plain plasterwork that gives the atmosphere of quiet and devotion we find today.

Brightly-coloured, even gaudy, representations of religious scenes would have met the eye if we entered these buildings in their early days. The atmosphere would have been more like that of an art-gallery or primary school class-room.

And with good reason. Where else could men's spirit be lifted by art and colour in those winter months when field and hill lay

Twelfth-century fresco of the Birth of John the Baptist in the chapel of St Gabriel, Canterbury Cathedral, Kent.

bare? In their way, the walls of these ancient churches provided colourful visual aids communicating God's truth.

Holy Trinity Church, Bosham, in Sussex, displays these ancient traditions. It is still possible to see the Saxon chancel arch, with stones dating from even before Augustine's arrival, going back to the later days of the Roman occupation of Britain.

The Saxon monasteries were great centres of Christian learning. We do not know the names of most of the monks, yet their treasures of devotion remain for us; works of great beauty, they testify also to the patient dedication of men representing God's holiness by the best that human art and skill could provide.

Paintings cover the walls of St Botolph's Church, Hardham, Sussex (AD 1050).

A decorated initial letter from the magnificently illuminated manuscript of the Lindisfarne Gospels.

The most beautiful book ever made

From eighth-century Ireland comes the volume that has been called 'the most beautiful book ever made', a manuscript of the four Gospels called *The Book of Kells*. Kells, in County Meath, had a long reputation for its learning. Now preserved in Trinity College, Dublin, *The Book of Kells* is a superb example of an illuminated manuscript. Each page is ornamented in gold, every sentence commences with an elaborately detailed letter testifying to the value placed on the living Word of God.

Another testimony to the skill and devotion of the monks can be seen in the *Lindisfarne Gospels,* now readily to be seen in the British Library, London.

Holy Island

Until its sacking by Vikings in the ninth century, Lindisfarne was a great centre of Northumbrian learning and education. It was shortly after the death of its great bishop, St Cuthbert (634-687), that the *Lindisfarne Gospels* were produced. A moment's reflection in front of these glorious pages lights up the so-called Dark Ages and assures us of the continuity in these islands of Christian learning.

Alfred of Wessex

Alfred King of Wessex (849-900) was a Christian of exceptional devotion. Decisively defeating Guthrum the Dane, he had the Danish army in his power and could have killed them to a man. Guthrum said it would be an honour to die at his hand, but Alfred said he knew a better way. He wished to win over his savage foe as a brother and live in peace. Alfred's translation of the first fifty Psalms reflects his feeling for King David's situation, so similar to his own. He took the Bible's teaching as the framework for his laws – setting English Law on Christian foundations.

Saintly Edward the Confessor (1003-66) gave us Westminster Abbey, and with his own palace nearby, set apart Westminster as the future centre of empire.

Freedom under the law

A great medieval archbishop, and the first Englishman of note to hold the position since the Norman Conquest, was Stephen Langton. Born c 1150 he left three separate legacies.

Most famously, it was Langton who supported the barons in their conflict with King John, but counselled a charter of rights rather than a bloody civil war. At the signing of Magna Carta in 1215 his name headed the list of counsellors. A biblical scholar, he drafted into the Charter the Christian ideal of freedom under the law which has inspired generations of Englishmen.

Seven years later he produced his rules, which are still an important part of the Church of England law. Interestingly, it was also Langton who was responsible for first organising the Old Testament into the now familiar chapters.

F lucas uirtulus 7

INcipit euangelium · · secundum lucam · · ·

QUO
NIAM
QUIDEM
MULTI
LISUNTORDINA
RENARRATIONEM

Gleaming spires

The Middle Ages saw the construction of many of the great cathedral churches which still today remain awe-inspiring and majestic.

The earlier cathedrals such as Durham, constructed by the Benedictine Order around the shrine of St Cuthbert, belong, like Canterbury itself, to the Romanesque style. This style is distinctive, with its rounded arches, lesser use of decoration and generally heavier mode of construction than became common in the later Gothic style of which Salisbury Cathedral, distinguished by its lofty spire, the tallest in England, is a fine example.

The west fronts of cathedrals were often utilised for a festival of decoration. One of the most awe-inspiring sights any cathedral in these islands has to offer is the great west front of Wells Cathedral. One can but marvel at the workmanship and devotion of masons of past centuries.

Gloucester Cathedral.

The famous west front of Wells Cathedral, Somerset.

Separate from the world

A number of cathedral churches were linked with or founded on the site of monasteries. The monastic ideal called for separation from the world and discipline to set the mind and will more firmly to obey God's word. It involved a life where work to support the community was combined with frequent hours at prayer.

No part of the British Isles was more richly provided with monasteries than Ireland. In the earlier centuries it had been Irish monks who spread Christianity throughout not only the northern part of Britain but also through much of Europe too.

After the Norman Conquest many of the feudal lords presented lands to the monasteries to help them support themselves, and until the sixteenth century many of the monasteries formed large and important communities.

The ruined shell of Fountains Abbey in the Wye Valley.

Mission to the towns

However, by the end of the twelfth century, many Christians were concerned that the isolated life of the monk, fine though it might be for the individual's soul, left the emerging townships without adequate spiritual leadership. So the debate between individual holiness and Christian social concern and teaching led to the founding of the several orders of friars.

Like monks, the friars dedicated themselves to a religious life. However, unlike the monks, they lived and worked among the ordinary people, teaching and preaching the gospel and performing works of charity. The different orders became known by the colour of their robes; for instance, the Dominicans or 'Black Friars' gave their name to the area of London north of the Thames where they settled in the thirteenth century.

The ruined church of Mount Grace Priory, Yorkshire.

The poet Geoffrey Chaucer
(c 1340–1400) is best known for
his *Canterbury Tales*.

A good parson

In the *Canterbury Tales*, written near the end of the fourteenth
century, Goffrey Chaucer presents us with a motley array of
pilgrims. Among this band are a number of churchmen and
women. For example the humble and impoverished parson:

> A good man there was of religion,
> Who was a poor Parson of a town,
> But rich he was of holy thought and work.
> He was also a learned man, a clerk,
> That Christ's gospel truly would preach,
> His parishioners devoutly would he teach.

Chaucer's parson is surely the pattern towards which all the great
founders and reformers of the church have striven.

Chaucer's age saw too the development of a form of drama in
which Christian teaching and English tradition were intermingled.
This was the Corpus Christi play, so called because it was tradi-
tionally performed on the medieval feast-day of Corpus Christi
(literally 'body of Christ'). Nowadays these plays are more usually
referred to as Mystery Plays.

Mixed together in these Mystery Plays were Christian teaching and comedy – a combination more readily accepted by the
medieval mind than today. For example in the Chester Play of
Noah, poor Noah has a very hard job to persuade his wife to leave
off gossiping and board the Ark!

The Virgin and Child, a panel
from a fourteenth-century
stained glass window in Eaton
Bishop parish church.

orsope you the ophile first I mad a sermoun or wou of alle þe þingis þat iesus bigan for to do & teche: til in to þe day in þe whiche he comaudede to þe apostlis bi þe hooly goost: who he chese was taken up. To whom & he ʒaue hym self alyue or quyc after his passioun. in mauy ar gumentis or preuyngis bi fourty days: apperynge to hem & spekynge of þe rewme of god. And he etynge to gydere comaudide to hem þat þei schulden not depte fro ierusalem but þei schulden þe abide þe biheeste of þe fadir: þe ʒe herden he seiþ bi my mouþ. So þely iohn baptizide in water: but ʒee schuln be baptisid in þe hooly goost: not after þes ma uy days. Therfore þei camen to gi dre: axeden hym seyinge. Lord ʒif in þis tyme: schalt þou restore þe kyngdom of israel. forsope he sei de to hem. It is not ʒoure for to haue knowe þe tymes or mome tis: þe whiche þe fadir haþ putte in his power. But ʒee schuln take þe vertu of þe hooly goost comynge fro aboue in to ʒou & ʒee schulibe witnessis to me in ierusalem in al ju dee and samarie: & vnto þe vtmeste of þe erþe. And whanne he hadde seide þese þinges hem seyinge: he was liftaup and acloude receyued hym fro þe eʒen of hem & whanne þei byheelden hym goyuge in to heuene: loo two men stoden biʒ bildis hem in whiit cloþis þe whiche aud seiden. men of galilee what stonden ʒee byholdinge in to heuene: þis iesus þat is take up fro ʒou in to heuene: so schal come as ʒee sawe hym goyuge into

heuen. Than þei turneden aʒen to ierim fro þe hill þat is clepid of olyuete þe whiche is bisidis ierusalem: hauynge þe iourneye of a saboth. And whane þei had den entride in to þe soupinge place þei wenten up in to þe lnʒer þinges wher þei dwelten petir & iohn ia mes & audrew philip & thomas. bartholomewe & mathu iames of alphey and symonzelotes: & iudas of iamys alle þes weren diwellinge or lastynge to gidre in preyer wt wymmen and marie þe moder of ie su and wt his breþeren. In þo dayes petir risyngeup in þe myd dil of breþeren: seide. forsoþe þere was a cumpanye of men to gidere: al meest an hundrid and twenty men breþeren it byhoueþ þe scripture to be fulfillid. whiche þe hooly goost before seide be þe mouþ of dauiþ. of iudas þat was leder of hem: þat token iesu þe whiche was nown brid in us: & gat þe sort of þis my nystre. And forsope þis weldide a feeld of þe hire of wickidnesse and he haugid to barst þe myddil: and alle his entrailis ben sched abrood & it was mad knowen to alle me dwellinge in ierusalem: so þat þe ille feeld was clepid achildemac in þe langage of hem: þat is þe feld of bloode. fforsope it is write in þe booke of psalmys. The habita cioun of hym be maad desert and be þer not þat dwelle in it: And an oþer take þe bischoprihe of hym/ þerfore it bihoueþ of þis me þat maad ben gadrid to gider wt vs in alle tyme in whiche þe lord iesu entride in & wente out amoug vs bygynnynge fro þe baptyme of iohn vnto þe day in whiche he was taken up fro vs: oon of þese for to be maad a witnesse

Upon this medieval scene of majestic cathedrals and mystery plays, but also growing superstition and spiritual darkness, came John Wycliffe (or Wyclif). Born in Yorkshire about 1330 in the reign of Edward III, he went to Oxford, a student aged sixteen, just as the terrible Black Death was destroying one-third of the entire population of Europe. Wycliffe's thoughts turned to things eternal and he started reading his Latin Bible. In his early thirties, Wycliffe became Master of Balliol College, Oxford. He said: 'My friend the hour has come, society is changing and the church is not changing with it. We ask God then, in his supreme goodness, to reform our church.' Condemned for his reforming zeal, he was tried for heresy at St Paul's Cathedral and later at Lambeth Palace. The first trial broke down in riot and the second was stopped by the Queen Mother.

Now Wycliffe saw that something deeper than reform was required. He took the tremendous step of translating the Bible into English. He said, 'Cristen men and wymmen, olde and yonge, shulden studie fast in the Newe Testament for it is of ful autorite, and opyn to undirstonding of simple men, as to the poyntis that be moost nedeful to salvacioun.'

He put the hand-written English scriptures in the hands of poor preachers who went throughout the country much as Wesley's preachers of a later century. Then, as Sir Winston Churchill comments; 'The spirit of early Christianity now revived the English countryside with a keen refreshing breeze.'

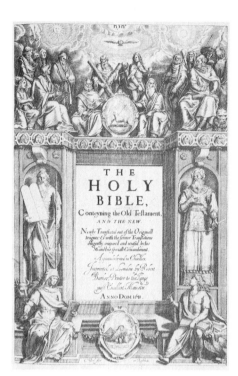

The title page of the first edition of the Authorised Version, 1611.

William Tyndale

Later others too were impelled to provide English translations of God's Word. William Tyndale was one. He determined to make the Bible available in the vernacular: 'Can one imagine a family where the children were unable to understand what their father says! If God spares my life, ere many years I will take care that a plough boy shall know more of the Scriptures than the Bishop in his palace.'

For his work, Tyndale was forced to leave England and work in Germany and the Netherlands. Assisted by Miles Coverdale, he translated the entire New Testament into English, basing his work on the Greek texts now available in the West. Since Wycliffe's time, printing too had been invented. Tyndale's New Testament reached these shores in 1526. Eventually he was betrayed and executed. At the stake he prayed: 'Lord, open the eyes of the King of England.'

Coverdale continued Tyndale's work and finished the first complete Bible to be printed in English. Coverdale's Bible was followed in 1539 by the *Great Bible,* and by the *Douai Bible* (1582).

The best-loved English Bible

All this work reached its culmination when in 1611 a committee of devoted scholars produced the *King James Version,* the *Authorised Version.* This has remained the most loved English Bible, for while the recent translations are more easily understood and provide more accurate versions of some passages, the *Authorised Version* is

This manuscript of the Wycliffe Bible once belonged to the younger son of Edward III.

magnificent in its beauty and splendid in the balance of its sentences. It has helped form the very language which we write and speak.

Reformation faith

From the Bible to the liturgy of the Church of England; modern services cannot rival for sheer beauty the work of one man who more than any other ensured that the liturgy would become an enduring part of the nation's faith and worship: Thomas Cranmer.

Architect of Anglicanism

Cranmer was born in 1489. He became Archbishop of Canterbury in 1533 and was the architect of the new Church of England. It was this godly man who insisted that every church in the land must contain a copy of the Bible in the language of the people – and who was responsible for the First and Second Prayer Books of 1548 and 1552.

The martyrdom of Thomas Cranmer. The Martyrs' Memorial at Oxford commemorates the deaths of Bishops Cranmer, Latimer and Ridley.

Cranmer's English is rich, balanced and clear, wonderfully fit to express the Christian faith. Here he speaks on 'The True, Lively and Christian Faith':

> This is the true, lively and unfeigned Christian faith and is not in the mouth and outward profession only, but it liveth and stirreth inwardly in the heart. And this faith is not without hope and trust in God, nor without the love of God and of our neighbours, nor without the fear of God, nor without the desire to hear God's word, and to follow the same in eschewing evil, and doing gladly all good works.

In the reign of Mary I Cranmer was arrested. He signed a document repudiating his former beliefs. Yet, when taken to Oxford in March 1556 to repeat his confession publicly, he refused to deny his beliefs. For his steadfastness to God's truth, he was burned at the stake. It is said he thrust his right hand directly into the flames, saying that it should burn first as the cause of his offence against the truth.

Archbishop Cranmer was largely responsible for shaping the Church of England after the English Reformation.

St Giles' Cathedral, Edinburgh.

Many martyrs

So Cranmer followed his faithful friends Bishops Latimer and Ridley, who had died with the prophetic words, 'We shall this day light such a candle, by God's grace, in England as I trust shall never be put out.' They spoke too for the nearly 400 who also suffered martyrdom in these troublous decades, Christian men and women of both humble and high estate.

One of these was Sir Thomas More, executed on Tower Hill. He was learned, a skilful lawyer, a writer whose *Utopia* describes a state untroubled by the evils of the day, and a politician who became both Speaker of the House of Commons and, in 1529, Chancellor, under King Henry VIII. His faith and integrity led him to take a firm stand 'for which he was duly executed'.

Scots reform

Meanwhile in the north, John Knox (1514–72) the fiery Scots reformer, restored the Bible to a central position in the Scots church. The way of reform had already been prepared by Lollard preachers and by the new biblical scholarship.

John Knox gave the Scots church a new Confession of Faith, a new Book of Discipline and a new Liturgy.

The reign of Elizabeth I (1559–1603) was one of the greatest periods of English history. It was also an age when Christian religious expression was of vital importance to many citizens.

This expression poured forth most beautifully in the church music of the age, and in none of its composers more than in Thomas Tallis and William Byrd.

Sir Thomas More. On the eve of his execution he wrote to his daughter: 'Praye for me, and I shall for you and all your freindes that we maie merily meete in heaven.'

John Knox's house, Edinburgh.

In 1607 the first permanent English-speaking colony in America was established at Jamestown, Virginia. At first landfall at Cape Henry, a wooden cross was erected and thanks returned to God for this new land. At Jamestown, Captain John Smith, the colony's governor, recalls their first church, 'we did lay an old saile to three or four trees to shadow us from the sunne: our walles were rales of wood, our pulpit a bar of wood nailed to two trees.' When later famine struck the Jamestown colony in their 'starving time' it was their chaplain, Robert Hunt who by selfless example held it all together.

A replica of the Mayflower moored in Plymouth, Massachusetts.

In 1620, the Pilgrim Fathers, sometimes called 'England's greatest living export', sailed for New England. The *Mayflower* was crowded with 102 people for her hazardous voyage to the Plymouth colony. On arrival they made the Mayflower Compact: 'Having undertaken for the Glory of God and advancement of the Christian Faith . . . a voyage to plant the first colony in the northern parts . . . do solemly, in the presence of God and one another covenant . . . to frame such just and equal laws . . .'

George Herbert's family came from Montgomery, Powys.

MUSICIANS AND POETS

Father of English music

Thomas Tallis, organist at Waltham Abbey, became organist and gentleman of the Chapel Royal. His special contribution was in his glorious musical settings of the English words for the main services of the church, a style much simpler than for the former Latin services. He has become known as the 'father' of English church music. William Byrd was Tallis' most famous pupil. He too became organist and gentleman of the Chapel Royal. His music is perhaps best heard in his famous 'Lullaby' and his *Masses* for Three, Four and Five voices, written during the 1590's.

Poets corner

More than any other era, the seventeenth century saw the writing of much poetry in which the English language was used with much imagination to describe Christian doctrine and experience.

Sir Walter Raleigh (1552-1618), Elizabethan mariner, explorer and poet wrote in his Bible:

> Who in the dark and silent grave,
> When we have wandered all our ways,
> Shuts up the story of our days.
> But from this earth, this grave, this dust
> My God shall raise me up, I trust!

Perhaps the finest religious poet of that age was George Herbert (1593–1633). Educated at Westminster School, he became Fellow of Trinity College, Cambridge. Though of aristocratic family, he became a priest and spent the last few years of his life in the country parish church of St Andrew, Bemerton, near Salisbury. Herbert saw the divine creation behind ordinary, everyday work.

> A man that looks on glass,
>   On it may stay his eye;
> Or, if he pleaseth, through it pass,
>   And then the heavens espy.

John Milton (1608–1674) epic poet, was Latin secretary to Cromwell. After the Restoration of Charles II in 1660 he produced his major work *Paradise Lost,* in twelve books, telling the story of the fall of Lucifer and the subsequent tempting of Eve and Adam. By the time he wrote this and the verse drama *Samson Agonistes,* Milton, like Samson, was blind.

> These are thy glorious works, Parent of good
> Almighty! thine this universal frame,
> Thus wondrous fair! Thyself how wondrous then!
> Unspeakable! who sitt'st above these Heavens
> To us invisible, or dimly seen
> In these thy lowest works; yet these declare
> Thy goodness beyond thought and power divine.
> *From 'Paradise Lost', Book V*

John Milton wrote a defence of free speech, including these words: 'Behold now this vast city (London); a city of refuge, the mansion house of liberty, encompassed and surrounded with God's protection.'

The faithful Quaker

Born the son of a weaver in Fenny Drayton, Leicestershire, George Fox (1624–1691) was always a serious-minded young man. He travelled widely to enquire of many preachers and in his early twenties started to preach himself. He enriched our Christian heritage by founding his Society of Friends, a group of people who would meet together to worship God in a simple and sincere way. Cynical critics picked on Fox's instruction to his people to tremble at the Word of the Lord, and members of the Society were nicknamed 'Quakers'. It is a tribute to the men and women who followed Fox that the name Quaker has long been held in high respect. They believed that buildings and ornaments were unnecessary for worship when the inner light of Christ dwells in the believer. Christ's words in the New Testament sufficed to guide the Christian.

The authorities of his day did not take kindly to his insistence on the Biblical principle. So, for no other reason than this, George Fox spent six years in different prisons in Nottingham, Carlisle, Launceston and Worcester. Those who knew him spoke of both his courage and his honesty. Quakers were later leaders in the abolition of slavery, the founding of Pensylvania Colony and our system of fixed-price trading – they held it wrong to ask a higher price than one was willing to take.

Bunyan's Progress

John Bunyan (1628–1688), one of the world's most widely-read Christian writers, was the son of a humble Bedfordshire tinker. At the age of nineteen he served in Cromwell's parliamentary garrison, but once free from military service he married and travelled the district on foot, mending cooking pots. Hearing some poor women who were sitting at a door discussing the things of God, he realised his own needs, and, in his search for the truth, joined the independent congregation at St John's Church, Bedford, whose pastor was John Gifford.

Bunyan discovered he had a gift for preaching, but in 1660, when the monarchy was restored, unauthorised preaching was forbidden in an attempt to enforce religious uniformity. Because he refused to be silenced, John Bunyan was imprisoned and spent the next twelve years in gaol.

Most of his time in gaol was spent writing, and from his pen flowed the words of *Grace Abounding to the Chief of Sinners* and *Pilgrim's Progress*. Bunyan was finally released from prison. He travelled and wrote about sixty books before he died of pneumonia while on a visit to London. He is buried in Bunhill Fields, but his Meeting House and Museum are situated in Bedford.

Here is the famous passage from *Pilgrim's Progress* describing Mr Valiant-for-Truth crossing the last river:

'Then said he, I am going to my Father's and though with

great difficulty I have got hither, yet now I do not repent me of all the troubles I have been at to arrive where I am. My sword I give to him that shall succeed me in my pilgrimage and my courage and skill to him that can get it. My marks and scars I carry with me to be a witness for me that I have fought His battles who now will be my rewarder . . . As he went he said, "Death where is thy sting?" and as he went down deeper he said, "Grave, where is thy victory?" So he passed over and all the trumpets sounded for him on the other side.'

Portrait of John Bunyan by Sadler, 1684/5.

Edinburgh Castle stands high on a rock that may once have been the site of an iron-age hillfort.

Covenanting Scots

The Covenanters were Scottish Presbyterians who, in the early 1600's resisted the Episcopal system being forced upon Scotland. Seeing the issue as obedience either to God or the king, they took to the moors and mountains, where thousands of people gathered to hear the Word of God preached and receive the sacraments. They were hunted, jailed and killed and some banished to Holland or America.

During the twenty-eight years' persecution, over 18,000 suffered hardship or death, and in the area of Greyfriars churchyard Edinburgh, where the National Covenant was signed in 1638, many martyrs are commemorated on the monument against the north wall. Here too is the site of the enclosure, where 1,200 Covenanters taken prisoner at the Battle of Bothwell Bridge were held for five months without shelter. The ancient motto of the Church of Scotland, *'Nec tamen Consumebatur'*, was verified now as evidently as ever: 'Behold the bush burned with fire, and the bush was not consumed'.

The distinctive skyline of
Edinburgh. The National
Covenant was signed here in
1638.

St Martin's in the Fields, the famous London church which stands overlooking Trafalgar Square.

If you seek my monument . . .

Where may more churches be seen closer together than in any other part of Britain? In the City of London; and overshadowing them all the dome of St Paul's.

Following the Great Fire of 1666, Christopher Wren was given a brief as wide in scope as any architect might dream of: 150 new churches and St Paul's, whose splendid dome recalls classical architecture, while the baroque towers at the west end are in the fashionable style of their day. However, inside, hidden within these features, are the elements of a Gothic-style church.

Wren and his famous pupil Hawksmoor were responsible for many of the fine churches of London, their lines providing a noble and calm atmosphere complementary to the quiet devotion of older parish churches and cathedrals throughout the land.

Despite intensive and prolonged bombing of the City of London, St Paul's Cathedral survived World War II.

Sir Isaac Newton believed the understanding of the Bible was more important than all his scientific studies.

Mathematical genius

Sir Isaac Newton (1642–1702) was a great scientist and a Christian. Born in 1642 in Lincolnshire, he early showed an aptitude for creating simple scientific devices – the sun-dial, for example, attracted young Isaac's attention. But later he was no longer content to remake for himself the ideas and discoveries of others.

In his study of the Old Testament he believed that God was a God of Law; thus in creation God would have made the physical universe to be governed by physical laws. Searching from this premise he discovered the laws of gravity and momentum. The make-up of white light, the reflecting telescope and mathematical calculus were also his discoveries or inventions. Thus he became known as the 'Father of Modern Science'. In his book *Principia Mathematica*, Newton wrote:

> This most beautiful system of the sun, planets and comets, could only proceed from the counsel and dominion of an intelligent and powerful Being, this Being governing all things . . . as Lord God.

Best-loved oratorio

Of the great variety of music on biblical subjects, none has attained the enduring fame of George Frideric Handel's *Messiah*. Charles Jennens wrote the libretto using the *Authorised Version* of the Bible and the psalms from the *Book of Common Prayer*. With great inspiration prophecy, narration, meditation upon the sufferings of Christ, the atonement and the ultimate triumph of the resurrection at the last trumpet are woven into a seamless whole by Jennens. *Messiah* was begun in 1741 and received its first performance as a charity occasion in the New Music Hall, Fishamble Street, Dublin, on 13 April 1742.

Improving society

In 1698 the Society for the Promotion of Christian Knowledge (SPCK) was founded, with the purpose of setting up charity schools. No fewer than 1,300 charity schools were started in its first twenty-five years:

> Why should not the poor, by being taught to read, be put into a capacity of making some improvement in moral and religious knowledge?

said Joseph Butler in 1745, urging the continued work of these schools against some people's feelings that education for the poor was a threat to stable society.

Robert Raikes, (1735–1811) a Gloucestershire journalist, whose statue now stands in the Embankment Gardens in London, is remembered for his great interest in neglected children and the school he set up in his Gloucester parish in 1780. He wrote an article about his work, and the idea became so popular that by 1789 organized Sunday Schools had spread to Wales, Scotland, Ireland and the USA, and in 1803 a Sunday School Union was founded.

George Frideric Handel, composer of *Messiah*.

Part of the original manuscript of *Messiah*.

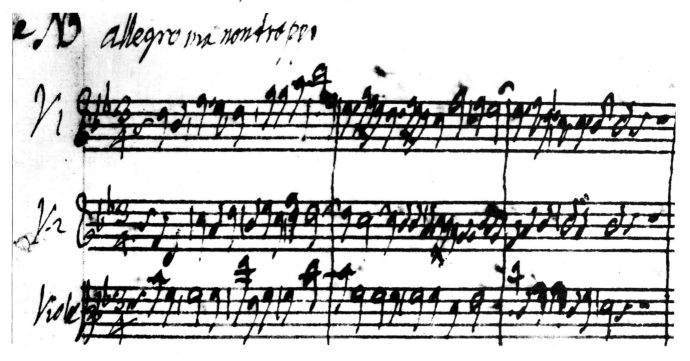

Stained glass window of Wesley preaching in the open-air, from the City Road Chapel, London.

This statue of John Wesley stands outside the City Road Chapel, London.

Methodical Christians

Three young clergymen, John and Charles Wesley and George Whitefield, met together while at Oxford University to pray and to live their lives methodically according to the New Testament. In 1735 John Wesley accepted an invitation to go to America.

'I went to America to convert the Indians, but, oh, who shall convert me?' Back at home again in London the answer came.

On Wednesday, 24 May 1738, John 'went very unwillingly to a society in Aldersgate Street where one was reading Luther's preface to the Epistle to the Romans. About a quarter before nine while he was describing the change which God works in the heart through faith in Christ, I felt my heart strangely warmed. I felt I did trust in Christ, in Christ alone for salvation and an assurance was given men, that he had taken away my sins, even mine, and saved me from the law of sin and death.'

It was with a new joy that John Wesley took the news of his faith to all who would hear him. Such joy that many clergymen, suspicious of enthusiasm, would not have him in their churches. This could not stop him preaching with such strong conviction of God's love and his plan for man's salvation. If he were not allowed into the pulpits, he would preach in the open air.

Thousands came to hear, many who felt the religion of the well-to-do was not for them. Experiencing transformed lives, they formed their own groups and became known as Methodists, sending preachers throughout the land. Before his death, John Wesley travelled some 250,000 miles, spoke to open-air meetings of up to 30,000, and preached some 40,000 sermons.

Great hymn-writers

Charles Wesley wrote many fine hymns which speak of his personal conviction of God's presence and love:

> O for a heart to praise my God,
>   A heart from sin set free;
> A heart that always feels thy blood
>   So freely spilt for me:
>
> A heart resigned, submissive, meek,
>   My dear Redeemer's throne;
> Where only Christ is heard to speak,
>   Where Jesus reigns alone.

Among many hundreds of other hymns, Charles wrote 'Hark, the Herald Angels Sing'.

John Newton, born in 1725, once deeply involved in the slave trade, turned to God during a violent storm at sea. In later years, as Curate of Olney in Buckinghamshire, he befriended the poet William Cowper and they produced the *Olney Hymns* including, 'Amazing Grace' and 'Oh, for a closer walk with God'. On becoming Vicar of St Mary Woolnoth in London he preached a famous series of sermons on the texts that Handel had used in *Messiah*. After one of these, it is said that William Wilberforce conferred with Newton, and that through his friendship with him was encouraged in his efforts to bring about the abolition of the slave trade.

The pulpit, City Road Chapel, London.

The Wesley brothers are both commemorated in this window in the City Road Chapel.

Expect great things

William Carey, who was born in 1761, became a Christian when he was 17 through the influence of John Warr, a fellow apprentice shoemaker in Hackleton, Northamptonshire. Carey became convinced that Christians were obliged to present the gospel to the heathen in other nations and he felt it right to take his family to India. He was taught Bengali by John Thomas on the journey by ship and first translated the Scriptures into this language before finally supervising translations into many other languages. He was also active in social reform, founded a leper hospital and pioneered horticultural work in India. He is remembered as the Father of Modern Missions and for a sermon in which he uttered the challenging words 'Expect great things from God; attempt great things for God'.

William Carey (1761–1834) devoted most of his life to taking the gospel to India.

Fighting slavery

William Wilberforce (1759–1833) fought over many years to right the terrible wrong of slavery. When his father died, he went to live with his aunt, a staunch Methodist. Wilberforce became the MP for the city of Hull (his birthplace). A few years later he met the great anti-slavery campaigner Thomas Clarkson and John Newton, a converted slave-trader. He determined to aid Clarkson's efforts against this appalling institution, then freely practised throughout the British Empire as well as in America. Wilberforce shook the commercial world with his attack on the slave trade. He said of his fellow Members of Parliament:

> They charge me with fanaticism. But if to be feelingly alive to the suffering of my fellow creatures is to be a fanatic, I am one of the most incurable fanatics of my age.

Their campaigning bore fruit in 1807 when Parliament passed an act forbidding the slavers to make use of British ports. While the act did much to extirpate the evil trade, it was of no help to existing slaves and their families. So in 1823 Wilberforce formed the Anti-Slavery Society. The act abolishing slavery in British colonies was passed in 1833, just before he died.

William Wilberforce, MP for Yorkshire, influenced prominent politicians quietly and persuasively.

Elizabeth Fry,
and fellow Quaker John Howard,
worked unceasingly to
improve the treatment of prisoners.

Prisoners, beggars and the homeless

Elizabeth Fry (1780–1845), the daughter of a Quaker banker, married Joseph Fry. At thirty-three she set out to investigate the stories she had heard about the inhumane treatment of women prisoners in London's Newgate Prison. She discovered that the prisoners often had their innocent children with them in the foul stench and vicious company of the cells.

Inspired by her love of God, she knew that mere wishes would achieve nothing and so she became deeply involved, providing decent clothes and education for the prison children. In 1817 she began to campaign for the separation of the sexes in gaol, classification of prisoners and many other reforms. She did not, however, confine her work to the prisons, but also did much for beggars and the homeless.

The children's Earl

And so, in our record of Christian service to society, we come to the Seventh Earl of Shaftesbury. For many years he sat in the House of Commons and in 1828 was involved with the reform of the Lunacy Laws (the insane, like the imprisoned, had previously been treated without humanity or understanding). Five years later he was campaigning for the first Factory Act. He championed the cause of women and children working in mines and in 1842 he helped bring the Mines Act on to the statute book. He pressed for an end to the abuse of using young children as chimney sweeps, to obtain improved housing for the poor, more humane treatment of young criminal offenders and to set up 'ragged schools' for the children of the poor. The 'Eros' statue in Piccadilly Circus, London, was erected in his honour.

Lord Shaftesbury, the eminent Victorian social reformer.

The Industrial Revolution brought new problems of child labour, poverty and homelessness to the great cities.

**Florence Nightingale
was brought up to a life of leisure
and comfort, which contrasted vividly
with the squalor she later saw
in the military hospital in Crimea.**

The Lady with the Lamp

Florence Nightingale at Scutari.

Florence Nightingale was born in 1830 and in her long life (she did not die until 1910) laid down the practical principles of modern nursing. She was actually born in Florence and must have seemed set fair for a life of ease and pleasure. Yet, not for the first time in this story, we find a young person feeling the call of God amidst personal comfort.

Victorian hospitals were quite unlike the hospitals of today; they were often ill-kept and filthy. Florence's parents were well aware of this; and strongly opposed their daughter's wish to work in such a place. Unable to become a nurse at once, she contented herself with visiting hospitals.

In 1853 Florence Nightingale became Superintendent of the Harley Street Hospital for Sick Gentlewomen, a respectable enough sounding post to our ears, but not to her parents'. Their unrelenting opposition continued, but her years of keen observation had not been wasted and the new superintendent's abilities soon became obvious.

News of the terrible sufferings of the wounded British soldiers in the Crimea came flooding home to Britain. Sidney Herbert, Secretary of State for War, was a friend of Florence and, aware of her courage and skill, he asked her to organise a group of women nurses to run the military hospital at Scutari in the Crimea.

Thirty-eight nurses, under Florence's leadership, set sail from England. The hospital they found was even dirtier than those Florence had seen in Britain. Yet within a short time Florence had reformed the place. All was made orderly; food, clothes, bedding and bandages provided. She made regular inspections of the wards by night, guided by her single light – 'The Lady with the Lamp'.

Dr Livingstone, I presume?

The story of the great Scottish missionary David Livingstone must be told, for his life was crammed with endeavour in the name of God. A son of a poor family in Blantyre, Lanarkshire, at the age of ten in 1823 he was set to work in a cotton mill. But he was determined to become a doctor and a missionary. He studied hard at night school and spent every spare minute at the mill also engrossed in books. Eventually in 1838 the London Missionary Society accepted him for training and he became a doctor in 1840.

Livingstone's first plan had been to take the gospel to China. Instead, he was sent into Africa and began his task, which he shared with his wife Mary, of setting up Christian mission bases, teaching the local people and attending to their needs. Livingstone explored continuously, locating the Zambesi River, and discovering and naming the Victoria Falls. He also discovered Lake Nyasa – and, close by, the route of the appalling Arab slave-trade chain-gangs. He fought this sordid trade with all his might, yet managed to retain the respect of even the slave-traders.

In 1872, by the shores of Lake Tanganyika, Livingstone and the American journalist Henry Stanley met. A year later, while kneeling at prayer, David Livingstone died. His body was carried across Africa, a journey of 1,500 miles, and then brought home for burial in Westminster Abbey.

So, in David Livingstone, we have another Christian through whose untiring energy and devotion to God the lives of many thousands of people were changed.

Some of the exhibits in the Livingstone Museum, Blantyre, Lanarkshire.

The impressive doorway of Westminster Cathedral, London.

I have a work to do . . .

Early in the nineteenth century came an attempt by a number of visionary young men to re-establish the sense of the church as a body, which they felt was being lost in an age of rapid social and material change. All around was the 'encircling gloom' of massive industrial development, stupendous growth of cities and the transport revolution of the Railway Age. The church was out of touch with the industrial age. John Henry Newman was referring to this when he said: 'I have a work to do in England'.

Newman determined to restore the true apostolic traditions of the early church. He hoped to inspire the church to higher spiritual ideals at a time when some clergy found their work little more than a means to a quiet and comfortable earthly existence, and when the vast factories were pouring out more and more articles that encouraged a materialistic outlook on life: He preached:

'Scripture is a refuge in any trouble . . .

Let us use it according to our measure.'

The beauty of holiness

On 14 July 1833 John Keble preached the Assize Sermon in Oxford. It was published under the title *National Apostasy*. The prophet Samuel had continued to pray for King Saul and his land when they had turned from the Lord. Keble urged the need to fight for Britain when it too seemed to be swallowing the church up in the state; and so the Oxford Movement was born.

Keble was an outstanding scholar of his generation. His ideas, and those of others like him, such as Newman, Edward Pusey and Hurrell Froude, were spread through the land by a series of ninety pamphlets, called *Tracts for the Times*.

Keble's book *The Christian Year* contains such well-known hymns as 'New Every Morning is the Love'. The chapel of Keble College, Oxford, is a fine example of the emphasis on the 'beauty of holiness' in the Oxford Movement.

The Oxford Movement had an enormous effect on religious life in Britain. Religious orders were founded for the first time since the sixteenth century, and there was a grand movement of dedicated young priests to preach in the industrial slums of the new cities.

The Salvation Army cares for the needy in society.

A young Salvation Army bandsman.

**William Booth, founder of
the Salvation Army.**

In darkest England

William (1829–1912) and Catherine Booth came from Methodist
stock but, one hundred years after Wesley, that movement found
William and Catherine's zeal hard to live with. In 1865 they established an independent mission in the East End of London. They
had a very practical concern for the poor, but at first progress was
slow. Then William Booth recruited his volunteer army – the
Salvation Army, whose soldiers devoted their leisure time to the
'salvation of others from unbelief, drunkenness, vice and crime'.
Opposition and persecution soon followed with over 600 brutal
assaults on his men and women in uniform in one year alone, but
the work and the uniformed street bands kept right on. The
'Darkest England' scheme, begun in 1891, was a plan to attain 'for
every honest Englishman' the standard of living of the London cab
horse! The Salvation Army Museum at Judd Street in London
captures the turn of the century atmosphere, while today the Army
flag flies in over eighty countries around the world.

THE LIGHT OF THE WORLD

'The Light of the World' – one of the most celebrated religious paintings.

Brotherhood of painters

The mid-nineteenth century saw a movement that produced one of the most popular and frequently reproduced religious paintings of all time.

Early in the century a group of artists who shared the ideal of creating a Christian art with a simple and direct energy of composition had been formed. Called the Nazarenes, their influence and aspirations were felt in this country through their effect on the Pre-Raphaelite Brotherhood. The Brotherhood, dating from 1848, was created by the painters William Holman Hunt, John Everett Millais and Dante Gabriel Rossetti. Their work shares a tremendous attention to detail, made the more apparent by clear design. Holman Hunt's celebrated painting 'The Light of the World' shows Christ with a lantern knocking on a door – the door to the human heart:

> Behold, I stand at the door and knock, and if any man hear my voice and open the door I will come in.

Prince of preachers

Another towering figure of the Victorian era was Charles Haddon Spurgeon (1834–1892), the 'prince of preachers'. Born in Kelvedon, Essex, he was converted at the age of sixteen at a Primitive Methodist Chapel. He became a Baptist pastor, and at the early age of twenty was called to New Park Street Baptist Chapel, Southwark, London. It was soon filled to overflowing, necessitating the building of the Metropolitan Tabernacle in 1859.

First for boys

Sir William Alexander Smith of Glasgow was the founder of the Boy's Brigade in October 1883. He realised how difficult it was to maintain order among unruly boys in his Sunday School and with the support of the minister of his church, the Rev Dr Reith – father of Lord Reith of the BBC – started this uniformed voluntary work amongst boys. At the Diamond Jubilee celebrations of the Brigade in 1943, King George VI spoke to a parade of 300 boys in the quadrangle of Windsor Castle and said, 'Your founder, Sir William Smith, builded better than he knew, for he started not only a great movement, but one from which all our present widespread youth training was destined to spring. I feel sure the B.B. will go from strength to strength because it is built on the twin pillars of religion and discipline and so is meeting two of the greatest needs of the present time.'

A noble dream

> Praise to the Holiest in the height,
>   And in the depth be praise,
> In all his words most wonderful,
>   Most sure in all his ways.

Boys' Brigade bandsmen.

The words come from Cardinal Newman's poem 'The Dream of Gerontius', being the chorus of angels' praise for the greatness of God. Stirring words to the heart of the Christian; yet more stirring when set to glorious music by Sir Edward Elgar, a deeply religious composer. In his work, the central truths of the faith are rendered with nobility and beauty:

> O wisest love! that flesh and blood,
>   Which did in Adam fail,
> Should strive afresh against their foe,
>   Should strive and should prevail.

Modern cathedrals

The present century has seen the building of two magnificent structures to the glory of God. Two new cathedrals, each distinctively modern in style, yet each devoted to combining the best in building and decorative skills.

Sir Basil Spence's new cathedral at Coventry is built right beside the ruins of the old, itself a victim of wartime bombing. The new cathedral opened in 1962 and many British artists worked to provide decoration that would speak to the world of today. Behind the high altar is Graham Sutherland's tapestry of Christ the King, while on the wall outside is the major sculpture by Sir Jacob Epstein of St Michael defeating the devil.

The Metropolitan Cathedral of Christ the King in Liverpool was built during the 1960s. Circular, a modern solution to the idea of spire or tower, it gives the impression that the entire structure is soaring towards heaven. Unusually, the high altar is placed in the very centre of the cathedral to bring as many people as possible close to the celebration of the mass.

The flying Scot

The recent film *Chariots of Fire* re-told the story of Scotland's 'most famous, most popular and best-loved athlete', Eric Liddell. Selected to run in the 100 metres at the 1924 Olympics in Paris, his heart sank when he saw the heats were scheduled for a Sunday. He held it to be God's day and said, 'I'm not running on a Sunday'. No amount of persuasion by team officials could move him, but he agreed to enter the 400 metres on another day instead. In the final he drew the outside lane and, on a hot Friday afternoon, went on to set a world record and win the gold medal.

In 1925, Liddell went as a missionary teacher of pure science and athletics to the staff of the Anglo-Chinese College in Tientsin, North China. In 1942 the province was over-run by Japanese armies, and all foreigners were interned in prison camps. Eric Liddell's kindness and love for his fellow prisoners in Weihsien made their lives more tolerable, but his health failed and he died on 21 February 1945.

Eric Liddell, hero of the film 'Chariots of Fire'.

Surprised by joy

C. S. Lewis was born in Belfast in 1898 and wounded in France in World War I. Returning to Oxford to continue his studies in philosophy and English literature Lewis' real struggle began. In his spiritual autobiography *Surprised by Joy* he wrote:

> You must picture me alone in that room at Magdalen night after night feeling the steady unrelenting approach of him whom I so earnestly desired not to meet. That which I feared had at last come upon me; perhaps that night I was the most dejected convert in England.
>
> In the Trinity term of 1929 I gave in and admitted that God was God and knelt and prayed. I did not then see what is the most shining and obvious thing, the divine humility which will open the high gates even to a prodigal who is brought in kicking, struggling and resentful, darting his eyes in every direction for a chance of escape.

Lewis went on to become the most popular defender of Christianity in the English-speaking world. His books have sold in millions and are said to have 'made righteousness readable'.

C S Lewis, the Oxford don who tried to 'make righteousness readable'.

CHRISTIAN HERITAGE

The people in this book are only a few of the countless thousands of believers who by their faith, compassion and obedience to the truth have given us our Christian Heritage.

Jesus lived in Palestine and scarcely travelled more than a few hundred miles. How could he influence a nation so far away?

The answer lies in his followers who testified to his resurrection and who were filled with the 'Spirit of the Living Christ'.

Through them, and the generations that followed, Jesus came to the British Isles.

'Remember your leaders, who spoke the word of God to you. Consider the outcome of their way of life and imitate their faith. Jesus is the same yesterday and today and forever.'
Hebrews 13:7–8.

If you have any enquiries about the Christian faith you can write to the Christian Enquiry Agency, London W1A 2BD.

Christian Heritage is sponsored by *The Trinity Trust,* an educational charity. If you wish to support this work, please write to: The Trinity Trust, 57 Duke Street, London W1M 5DH.

Picture acknowledgments

Art Directors Photo Library 32
BBC Hulton Picture Library 28, 48, 51, 62, 63
British Museum 18, 19, 26, 27, 43
Tim Dowley 13, 21, 22/23, 23
Sonia Halliday 12, 14, 16/17, 17, 25
Keble College, Oxford 61
National Portrait Gallery 24, 29, 30, 35, 37, 42, 45, 49, 50, 52, 53, 57, 59
Salvation Army 58 (top)
Scottish Tourist Board 6, 7, 10/11, 31, 38/39, 39, 54, 55
Clifford Shirley 58 (bottom)
Mark Shrimpton 60
Wales Tourist Board 3, 9, 15, 34
Peter Wyart 4, 5, 8, 20, 40, 41, 44, 46, 47, 56, Cover